Nebraska

A Buddy Book
by
Julie Murray

ABDO
Publishing Company

VISIT US AT
www.abdopub.com

Published by ABDO Publishing Company, 4940 Viking Drive, Edina, Minnesota 55435.

Copyright © 2006 by Abdo Consulting Group, Inc. International copyrights reserved in all countries. No part of this book may be reproduced in any form without written permission from the publisher. Buddy Books™ is a trademark and logo of ABDO Publishing Company.

Printed in the United States.

Edited by: Sarah Tieck
Contributing Editor: Michael P. Goecke
Graphic Design: Deb Coldiron, Maria Hosley
Image Research: Sarah Tieck
Photographs: Clipart.com, Creatas, David Kaiser, Digital Vision, Getty Images, Library of Congress, One Mile Up, Photodisc, Photos.com

Library of Congress Cataloging-in-Publication Data

Murray, Julie, 1969-
   Nebraska / Julie Murray.
      p. cm. — (The United States)
   Includes index.
   Contents: A snapshot of Nebraska — Where is Nebraska? — All about Nebraska — Cities and the capital — Famous citizens — Pioneer Day — The land of Nebraska — Nebraska's weather — A history of Nebraska.
   ISBN 1-59197-686-3
      1. Nebraska—Juvenile literature. I. Title.

F666.3.M87 2006
978.2—dc22

                                                         2005045738

Table Of Contents

A Snapshot Of Nebraska

When people think of Nebraska, they think of its land. About 95 percent of Nebraska's land is used for farms. Nebraska farmers grow crops such as corn, wheat, and soybeans. They also raise cattle and hogs. This state is one of the top farming states in the United States.

Corn is one of many crops grown in Nebraska.

There are 50 states in the United States. Every state is different. Every state has an official nickname. Nebraska is called "The Cornhusker State." The term "cornhusker" means to harvest or "husk" corn by hand.

Some Nebraska farmers raise pigs.

Nebraska became the 37th state on March 1, 1867. The state is 77,359 square miles (200,359 sq km). It is the 15th-largest state in the United States. Nebraska is home to 1,711,263 people.

Where Is Nebraska?

There are four parts of the United States. Each part is called a region. Each region is in a different area of the country. The United States Census Bureau says the four regions are the Northeast, the South, the Midwest, and the West.

Four Regions of the United States of America

ALASKA

WASHINGTON

MONTANA

NORTH DAKOTA

MINNESOTA

VERMONT

MAINE

OREGON

IDAHO

WYOMING

SOUTH DAKOTA

WISCONSIN

MICHIGAN

NEW
YORK

NEW
HAMPSHIRE

MASSACHUSETTS

RHODE ISLAND

CONNECTICUT

PENNSYLVANIA

NEW JERSEY

NEVADA

UTAH

COLORADO

NEBRASKA

IOWA

ILLINOIS

INDIANA

OHIO

DELAWARE

Washington D.C.

MARYLAND

CALIFORNIA

KANSAS

MISSOURI

WEST
VIRGINIA

VIRGINIA

ARIZONA

NEW MEXICO

OKLAHOMA

ARKANSAS

KENTUCKY

TENNESSEE

NORTH CAROLINA

SOUTH
CAROLINA

MISSISSIPPI

ALABAMA

GEORGIA

TEXAS

LOUISIANA

FLORIDA

HAWAII

	West		Midwest		South		Northeast

Nebraska is located in the Midwest region of the United States. Nebraska has four seasons. The seasons are spring, summer, fall, and winter. Nebraska can have severe weather. This includes flooding in the spring, tornadoes in the summer, and blizzards in the winter.

Blizzards can make it hard to see.

Nebraska borders six other states. South Dakota is to the north. Iowa lies to the east. Missouri borders the southeast corner. Kansas is south. Colorado borders the state in the southwest corner. Wyoming is west.

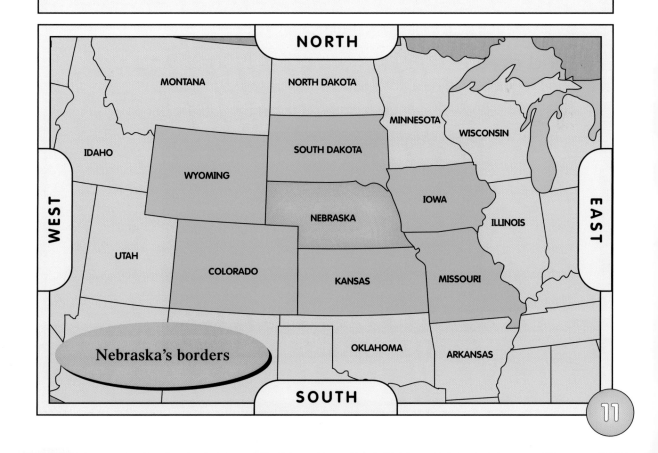

Nebraska's borders

Nebraska

State abbreviation: NE

State nickname: The Cornhusker State

State capital: Lincoln

State motto: Equality Before the Law

Statehood: March 1, 1867, 37th state

Population: 1,711,263, ranks 38th

Land area: 77,359 square miles (200,359 sq km), ranks 15th

State flag:
Adopted in 1925

State tree: Cottonwood

State song: "Beautiful Nebraska"

State government: Three branches: legislative, executive, and judicial

Average July temperature: 76°F (24°C)

Average January temperature: 23°F (-5°C)

State flower: Goldenrod

State bird: Western meadowlark

State animal: White-tailed deer

Cities And The Capital

Lincoln is the capital city of Nebraska. The inside of Nebraska's Capitol features murals showing the state's history. Outside the Capitol, there is a statue called *The Sower*. It sits on top of a gold dome. This statue represents the importance of farming in Nebraska.

The Nebraska State Capitol is one of only four in the United States that is designed like a skyscraper. It cost just under $10 million and took 10 years to build.

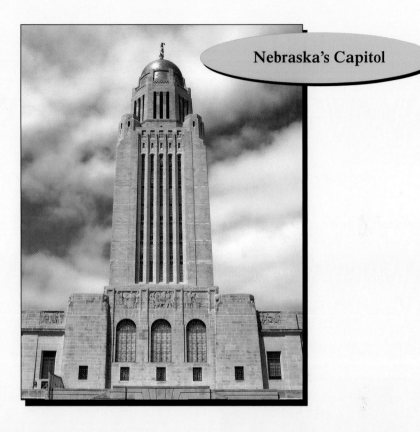

Nebraska's Capitol

Omaha is the largest city in Nebraska. Omaha became a city in 1857. It was once considered a "Gateway to the West." Today, Omaha is a major transportation and agricultural center.

Famous Citizens

Gerald Ford (1913–)

Gerald Ford was born in Omaha in 1913. On December 6, 1973, he was appointed vice president of the United States. On August 9, 1974, President Richard Nixon resigned. When this happened, Ford became the 38th

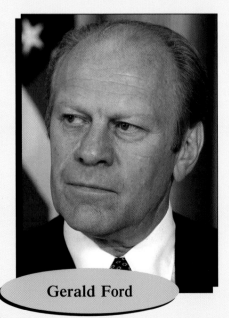

Gerald Ford

president. Ford served as the president of the United States from 1974 to 1977. He is the only person to be president and vice president without being elected.

Famous Citizens

Fred Astaire (1899–1987)

Fred Astaire was born in Omaha in 1899. Astaire was famous for his dancing. He was also an actor and a singer. He starred in many musicals. Ginger Rogers was his most popular on-screen partner. They appeared in 10 movies together.

Fred Astaire

Pioneer Days

Thousands of pioneers crossed through Nebraska while heading west in the 1800s. Back then, the western part of the United States was a great wilderness. They traveled on the Oregon Trail. The Oregon Trail extended from Missouri to Oregon.

Men, women, and children traveled in covered wagons across the open plains of Nebraska. Herds of buffalo roamed the land.

Chimney Rock was one famous landmark along the Oregon Trail. Pioneers could see the towering rock formation for miles. Today, it is a national historic site.

A view of Chimney Rock.

In 1862, President Abraham Lincoln signed the Homestead Act of 1862. This made it a law. The act said people could have 160 acres (65 ha) of public land for free. The land was available to any person who was the head of a household and at least 21 years old. This brought thousands of settlers to Nebraska. Today, people can visit the Homestead National Monument of America in Beatrice.

Daniel Freeman was the first homesteader in Beatrice. His home is the site of the Homestead National Monument.

The Land Of Nebraska

The land of Nebraska gently rises across the state from east to west. The eastern part of the state is often called the Central Lowlands. This area has rich farmland and many streams and rivers. All of these flow into the Missouri River.

Omaha is near the Missouri River in the Central Lowlands area.

The middle and western parts of the state are called the Great Plains. The Sand Hills are part of this area. The Sand Hills are blanketed with grasses. Streams and underground water make this a great area for ranching. The sand hills cover about 20,000 square miles (51,800 sq km) of land. This is the largest area of sand dunes in America.

Scott's Bluff National Monument
is in western Nebraska.

The highest point in the state is Panorama Point. It is found in western Nebraska. It rises 5,424 feet (1,653 m) above sea level. On a clear day, people can see the Rocky Mountains to the southwest.

Nebraska's Weather

A rainstorm over the plains of Nebraska.

Nebraska's weather changes often. Springtime in Nebraska is unpredictable. It can be warm and sunny one minute and cold and hailing the next.

The summer months are typically hot and humid. Flooding rains, thunderstorms, and tornadoes are common.

Tornadoes form when hot, humid air and cool, dry air meet. When tornadoes form, homes and cities can be damaged. This is because the swirling funnel cloud moves very fast and the winds are very strong.

Nebraska has good weather, too. In the spring and summer months, it is warm. This weather helps to grow crops.

A farm in Nebraska covered with snow.

Winters in Nebraska are often cold and windy. The state gets an average of 30 inches (76 cm) of snow each year. Strong winds blow across the open prairies and farmland creating blizzards.

Nebraska

1714: Étienne Veniard de Bourgmont arrives in Nebraska. He is the first recorded European in the state.

1803: President Thomas Jefferson arranges for the United States to buy Nebraska as part of the Louisiana Purchase.

1804: Explorers Meriwether Lewis and William Clark reach the eastern edge of Nebraska.

1819: The United States Army builds Fort Atkinson. Nebraska's first school is built here.

1854: The Kansas-Nebraska Act creates the Nebraska Territory.

1867: Nebraska becomes the 37th state on March 1.

1875: Nebraska adopts a new state constitution.

1937: Nebraska's unicameral (one-house) legislature meets for the first time.

1939: Oil is discovered in southeastern Nebraska.

1967: Nebraska celebrates its centennial.

1986: Kay Orr is the first woman to be elected governor of Nebraska.

2005: Burwell hosts its 84th annual Big Rodeo.

Governor Kay Orr

Cities In Nebraska

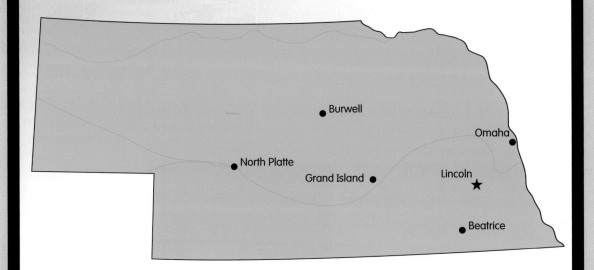

Burwell

Omaha

North Platte

Grand Island

Lincoln

Beatrice

Important Words

blizzard a heavy snowstorm with strong winds.

capital a city where government leaders meet.

centennial 100-year anniversary.

humid air that is damp or moist.

Louisiana Purchase a deal where the United States bought land from France. Part of this land later became Nebraska.

nickname a name that describes something special about a person or a place.

pioneers people who traveled across the United States in the 1800s to settle the western United States.

tornado a storm cloud that is shaped like a funnel and swirls fast, destroying homes and cities.

wilderness wild, unsettled land.

Web Sites

To learn more about Nebraska, visit ABDO Publishing Company on the World Wide Web. Web site links about Nebraska are featured on our Book Links page. These links are routinely monitored and updated to provide the most current information available.

www.abdopub.com

Index